GOD'S GENERALS

FOR KIDS

WILLIAM SEYMOUR

GOD'S GENERALS

FOR KIDS

WILLIAM SEYMOUR

BY
ROBERTS LIARDON
& OLLY GOLDENBERG

BRIDGE
LOGOS

Newberry, FL 32669

Bridge-Logos
Newberry, Florida 32669 USA

God's Generals For Kids — William Seymour
Roberts Liardon & Olly Goldenberg

Copyright ©2014 Roberts Liardon & Olly Goldenberg
Reprint 2020

Printed in the United States of America.

Library of Congress Catalog Card Number: 2014953413

International Standard Book Number 978-1-61036-206-1

Unless otherwise noted, all Scripture is from the King James Version of the Bible.

The photographs used are owned by and taken from the private collection of Roberts Liardon.

Timeline illustrations by David Parfitt.

WILLIAM SEYMOUR

CONTENTS

TIMELINE

1870

May 2
1870
Born

November
14, 1891
Dad dies

CHICAGO

1900

1891
Moves
north to
find a job

1891

1891

1900
To Chicago

1902
To Texas

April 1906
To Los
Angeles

April 9
1906
Pentecost
breaks out
in Bonnie
Brae

1902

April 9, 1906

1908

April 14
1906
Azuza
Street
meetings
begin

May 13
1908
Marries
Jennie
Moore

1922

September
28, 1922
Goes to
heaven

April 14, 1906

CHAPTER 1

BOTTOM OF THE PILE

William Seymour

"YOU WILL NEVER DO ANYTHING GREAT"

Have you ever wondered what you will do when you are older? Some people know they are born for greatness. Others are told,

"You are nothing special. You will never do anything special." Words like this can make a person feel very small, but God has planned something special for your life no matter what anyone else says or thinks.

When William Seymour was born *nobody* expected him to do anything great, not even his parents. You see William was born in America on May 2, 1870, and William was black.

His parents had both been slaves. His grandparents had also been slaves. Nearly all the black people were slaves. They were treated like pieces of property, not human beings. They were beaten and sworn at by everyone.

In 1857, a few years before William was born, the government had passed a law to say that nobody was allowed to own slaves anymore. The slaves hoped things would improve for them. Unfortunately things got worse not better.

"Just because were not allowed to own slaves, doesn't mean we have to like them," the slave owners said.

When the white people had slaves, all their work was done for them. Now if they wanted anything done they had to pay people to do it. Farms could not harvest the food anymore and started to shrink. There weren't many jobs for the ex-slaves. Not only were they still hated and badly treated, now they didn't even have work to do or food to eat.

Those who did have a job were not much better off. At the start of a year black people had to choose who they were going to work for that year. If they did anything wrong then they would lose their whole year's wages! They were no longer *called* slaves, but they were still *treated* like slaves.

These people were thought to be second class humans, just because of the color of their skin. The second class humans were really the ones who were treating them so badly.

CONTROLLED BY FEAR

Every day the ex-slaves lived in fear. People hated them and the law was against them. Laws were passed all over the land, known as the "Jim Crow" laws. These laws made sure that black people were not seen as people, but could be treated like animals.

Different races were not allowed to study at the same schools or even sit in the same parts of a bus. Everything was done to keep people with different skin colors away from each other. In one place over one hundred and fifty black people were shot for no reason.

Where William was born, in Centerville Louisiana, the people were filled with hatred against the blacks and because he was a black child, people spat at him and cursed him wherever he went.

With all the hatred in the world you would have thought that this was a great chance for the Church to be different. They could have shown how much God loves all people. They could have loved the people that everyone else hated, just like Jesus did when He was on Earth.

Sadly most churches failed to do this. In fact they didn't even let the black people into the building!

Many church goers even joined hate groups like the *Klu Klux Klan*. They used threats, violence and murder to show people that the white people were the best.

It takes a lot of courage to stand up to such hatred. Many people were not willing to do that. But even though William had a hard life, and nobody expected him to do anything, God had big plans for his future.

A SPIRITUAL UPBRINGING

Like many families, William's household was very spiritual. The slaves sang spiritual songs to help them cope with the torture. As they worked they would sing songs to God. But not many of them knew God personally as their Savior. William was excited by the spiritual life around him. As a young man he saw visions and he had been taught that Jesus was coming back to the Earth.

As William saw his friends beaten and killed, he knew that he could not do anything to stop them. The only person he could turn to was God. He would pray and ask God to bring justice. But he also did not yet know God as his Savior.

That's pretty much all we know about William's childhood.

It's hard to know much more about his young life. After all he was the son of slaves. The people who lived around him would never even think of writing about his life. They would only think, "Who would ever want to know anything about him?" Nobody kept a record of his life and William himself could hardly read or write.

For the same reason we know very little about his family. He had 9 brothers and sisters, but six of them died before they grew up. We can guess what it was like for them, because we know how badly the ex-slaves were treated.

When William was thirteen his dad became sick. As he lay on his bed the family called for a doctor to come, but the doctor didn't bother to show up. They called for a minister, but the minister did not get there in time. That night his dad died.

To most of the people around it was just the death of another ex-slave. But to William, his dad's death changed the whole family. His mom was now alone in the world and had to earn money to feed her family. They were so poor that they often did not eat.

TIME TO MOVE NORTH

Around this time William decided to move north to find work. Although he was only thirteen most people would be expected to be working full-time by this age, especially if they were poor and black. After all he was only allowed to learn a little bit. At this point in history, the white people did not want the black people to get too educated.

Loads of other black people were moving north. They had heard that people were treated better in the North and they could actually get jobs!

Getting as far as Memphis, Tennessee, William stayed with family friends. He got a job delivering groceries for a local shop to people's homes. It must have been nice for him to be a part of a family again. But soon after he arrived there, the dad of the home died.

William had no choice. He could not run away from death. He had to decide to keep on going. He was going to do something with his life!

When difficult things happen to us we can either let them stop us from doing anything or we can decide to fight on. William was not going to give up. He left his job as a porter and became a truck driver for a newspaper company, delivering newspapers.

A couple of years later he decided to move from Memphis to St. Louis. For the next few years he traveled to many different cities looking for jobs. He worked in bars, hotels and shops. He was willing to work anywhere that would give him a job.

But he was not happy with his life, so he kept on traveling, looking for answers. He didn't really know what he was doing in life. He just wanted to be accepted, not hated.

By the time he was twenty-five he had traveled as far as Indianapolis. He got a job as a waiter in a hotel. Life this far north was definitely better. He was earning more than twice as much as he could down south for doing the same job. He had to pay more for his rent just because he was black, and life was still not easy, but at least there was hope in this place.

Most of the black people at the time did not really plan to do anything great with their lives. After so many people told them that they could not do anything, most of them believed it was true.

As William looked around he saw black people who were professionals. These people had not only learned to read and write, they had also worked hard. All of William's jobs involved him serving other people, but these people were the leaders. Some of them were top business men in the city, others worked as doctors.

He began to think he could do something more than be a slave. Perhaps there was hope. So far in his life he had moved around a lot, trying to avoid trouble and places where there was political unrest. Now he saw his first glimmer of hope. Soon William was going to find far more hope than he had ever imagined possible.

CHAPTER 2

HOLINESS AND SICKNESS

Charles Parham, leader of William Seymour's Bible school

CALLED TO GOD'S KINGDOM

While in Indianapolis he went to an all-black Methodist church. These people accepted him and became like a new family.

During this time, William realized that Jesus had died for *him*. Before this time he knew Jesus had died for his people's sins; now he saw that Jesus had died for *his* sins. William repented of his sins and received Jesus' forgiveness straight away. He chose to follow God. This was what he had been looking for.

Now he knew God, he wanted to meet with other people who also knew God personally. He looked around and found a group called the Evening Light Saints.

These people spoke a lot about being holy like God is. They were part of a new type of church called the Holiness church. They did not wear rings or make up. They did not use musical instruments. They didn't dance or play cards. It may sound like they didn't have fun, but they were really happy.

The church reached out to all kinds of people, whether they were rich or poor, young or old, or even white or black. People from lots of different nations met and worshiped God together. William started to see that God doesn't care about the color of your skin. He only cares about what is going on in your heart.

If William had any doubts about following God they didn't last long. In this church everyone was seen as equal before God, and William, now with his sins forgiven, finally found peace and happiness.

CALLED IN GOD'S KINGDOM

While William was with the Evening Light Saints he felt God calling him to the ministry. He didn't dare answer God. He was a son of a slave. He could hardly read and write. How could God ever use him?

For weeks William felt God calling him to the ministry. For weeks William did not feel he could do it. Then one evening he started to feel unwell. His temperature went up and his skin started to break out in spots. William had caught small pox.

Back in the 19th century small pox was a really serious disease. Many people died from a small pox attack.

William survived it.

When he was well again he knew he had to obey God and do what God had called him to do.

The small pox had caused one of his eyes to become blind. It had also left scars like small pits all over his face so William grew a beard to hide them.

The disfigured, one-eyed son of slaves agreed to obey God.

TRAVELLING TOWARDS HIS DESTINY

William continued to travel. In 1900, he moved to Chicago where he worked as a waiter. He also spent a lot of time with the holiness churches. He was finding out more about God and God's fiery Word was now burning inside him.

In Chicago he also heard about a man called John Alexander Dowie (you can read his story in God's Generals for Kids, Volume 3). Mr. Dowie believed that all people were equal in God's Kingdom. In fact he didn't just believe it, he lived it. His church was full of thousands of people from different backgrounds who worshiped God freely together. Mr. Dowie also believed in divine healing. Many of the people in his church had been healed by God.

The more William heard the more excited he got. William just wanted to obey God, no matter what.

THE BAPTISM OF THE HOLY SPIRIT

As he got to know more about God, William knew it was time for him to train to be a minister. So he moved to Cincinnati and went to the Holiness Bible School there.

The holiness movement recognized that God had called him to the ministry. They did not care about how well he could read and write, or how much he knew. Instead they wanted to make sure that God had called him and that he was following God with all his heart. William clearly was. So in 1902 he was ordained as a minister in the Holiness church.

When William heard that his family had moved to Houston, Texas, he was desperate to join them. He had not seen them since he was young and after all his traveling he longed to be back with them again.

Traveling to Houston he looked all around for them. But God had somebody else that he wanted William to meet, Lucy Farrow.

Lucy was the minister in a Holiness Church. She asked William to join her. It was a great way for William to start his ministry, by helping Lucy to lead. William didn't know that he would soon be running the church.

Lucy felt that God wanted her to go and work for a preacher in Kansas. When she left, she put William in charge. It was his first proper church and he really enjoyed leading and caring for the people.

As he worked in the church, Lucy was working for a man who would change William's life forever. His name was Charles Parham (God's Generals for Kids, Volume 6). Charles had started a movement called the Apostolic Faith Movement and everyone was talking about what God was doing through him.

God had poured out His Holy Spirit on the people in the Bible School. It was an awesome experience. All through the church people were talking about this new baptism of the Spirit. "God seems to be doing the same things that He did in Acts 2," they said. People called it a modern day Pentecost.

Many of the people started to speak in tongues. Their language was strange. Sometimes they were speaking in a heavenly language. Other times they spoke a language from Earth that they had never learned.

"We thought we had been baptized in the Holy Spirit," they said. "But now we are not so sure. These people have something that we do not have."

Of course some people laughed at them and others said it was not from God. But God showed people that it really was Him.

When Lucy returned she told William all about it.

"I have been baptized in the Holy Spirit." She told him. "And now I can speak in tongues. You can be baptized too William."

"But I've already been baptized in the Spirit." William protested. "After all I am living my life for God. Why do I need this speaking in tongues thing?"

Most of the Evening Light Saints thought it was a load of nonsense. William wanted to know what God thought about it. So he got on his knees and prayed.

"Lord, I only want to believe what is from you. But I do not want to miss anything that you have for me. Please empty me of every false idea and show me what is true."

As William prayed and studied the Bible he saw that this baptism was another work from God. It was something that he did not have and he needed to ask God for it. William could see that something special had happened to Lucy and now he wanted the same experience too.

So, when Charles Parham came to Texas to lead some meetings, William went to every single one of them.

OFF TO BIBLE SCHOOL

Charles Parham decided to open a Bible School in Texas because he found so many people were hungry for God there. William really wanted to join it. But there was just one problem.

He was black. The Bible School was for white people only.

Charles Parham did not realize that God wanted all the nations to be together as equals. He believed that the black people needed the Gospel, but he thought that they were not as important to God as white people. (Perhaps that's why God didn't use Charles Parham to spread the message of Pentecost, but instead he chose a half-blind black man to do the job.)

Charles saw that William was really hungry for God.

"I'll tell you what we'll do," Charles said. "You can sit just outside the classroom and I will leave the door open while we teach." The "Jim Crow" laws meant that William was not allowed to study in the same room as the other students and Charles Parham did not want to go against this evil law.

So each day, William would sit next to the door and listen to all that was being said in the classroom.

When Charles went to the black parts of town he would take William with him. Even in these meetings the black people had to sit at the back, away from the white people. This was not the vision that William had seen. God wanted people from all nations to be together.

Charles and William were good friends, but they disagreed on a lot of things. Charles even refused to pray for William to receive the Holy Spirit.

We could judge Charles for this, but God still used him to help William. After all God is always bigger than our mistakes! William was about to be sent by God to Los Angeles where one of the greatest revivals of the century was about to take place.

CHAPTER 3

THE CITY IS GETTING READY

William Seymour studying the Bible

PEOPLE IN PLACE

When God is about to do something big, He always lets His people know about it. In fact, God plans everything perfectly. God gets each person ready and puts them in place ·

for His work, just like when you connect together pieces of a jigsaw puzzle to complete it.

Meanwhile, in the country of Wales there was an amazing revival that was changing the whole nation. Evan Roberts was one of the main leaders of the revival. People traveled from all over the world to meet Evan and to see the revival for themselves. You can read about this revival in God's Generals for Kids, Volume 5.

A man named Frank Bartleman wrote to Evan Roberts several times asking for prayer. "Please pray for us here in New York. I know God is going to bring a great revival here. Please pray that we will see the same things happening here that are happening in Wales."

Each time Evan would write back "I am praying for you all. Keep on going."

Pastor Joseph Smale was a local pastor in Los Angeles. He traveled all the way to Wales to see what God was doing there. When he came home he was different. God had changed something inside of him. Now he really wanted to see the same thing happen in his church and home town as well.

He started to hold meetings every night, calling people to come back to God. Frank Bartleman went to the meetings.

Sometimes Pastor Smale was late. When this happened, the people just sat around waiting for him.

"What are you all waiting for?" Frank asked. "We're not waiting for Pastor Smale, we're waiting for Jesus and He is already here. Let's pray."

As he started to pray others joined in, until people were on their faces crying out for God to move among them. By the time Pastor Smale arrived the people were already meeting with God.

Bit by bit, God was stirring something up in the people.

DO YOU WANT REVIVAL?

Of course not everyone wanted God to move. When God moves, things have to change. It can be hard work and it can be uncomfortable too, especially if people don't want to change.

Some of the people in Pastor Smale's church got tired of the revival meetings. "Can you stop them?" They asked him.

"No. I'm not going to stop what God has started." He replied.

The church gave him a final challenge: "Stop the meetings or stop being the pastor of this church."

Now Pastor Smale had a huge decision to make. He knew God had started these meetings, he knew that something special was going to happen. But he had not realized that it was going to cost him his whole ministry. He had to decide whether he was willing to give up the church and his salary to continue the meetings.

In the end he decided to trust God and obey Him. He left the church and started a new one. 190 people also left the church to join him. They wanted to be part of what God was doing too. People came and joined them from all over the city. God was bringing together the people who really wanted to meet Him.

GOD RAISES UP HIS PEOPLE

Many church members just wanted to go to the meetings to have a nice time and be blessed. But Frank Bartleman didn't want a nice time. He wanted an encounter with God. He was tired of the playing around in church. He was desperate for something more, he wanted people to connect with God. So he worked hard and prayed for God to move.

And he wasn't the only one.

All over the city more and more people were starting to meet together to cry out to God for something more. God wanted to do something in Los Angeles, so He was getting His people ready.

It may not have been a lot of people at this stage, but God doesn't need large numbers to do great things. After all, in the Bible Gideon was able to defeat a huge army with just 300 soldiers (and God). Jesus turned the world upside down starting with only twelve people (and His Holy Spirit).

The same thing was starting to happen here.

READY FOR REVIVAL

God's people were not only praying, but they were also going from one house to the next, telling people about Jesus. It was clear that they were ready for a revival, where many people would turn to God.

One group had just left their local Baptist church. Mrs. Hutchinson had preached strongly about the need to be holy. "God gives you grace to be saved, but it does not stop there. There is a second grace that God gives—the grace to be holy. We need to ask God for this second grace just like we asked Him to save us."

Her preaching was so strong that the Baptist church did not want her to stay with them anymore. The leaders did not agree that God wanted to make people live holy lives and they could see that people in the church were starting to listen to her teaching. So they asked her to leave.

As she left a number of the people left with her. Together they started a new mission on Santa Fe Street with her as their leader. Mrs. Hutchinson spoke with her relative Neely Terry, "You know Neely, the work is going well. But I think we need to have a male leader to help minister to the people."

Neely soon knew just who to ask.

A DIVINE MEETING

Neely travelled to Houston to visit some friends. While she was there she went to William Seymour's church. As William taught about the baptism of the Holy Spirit she realized that this was what they needed in Los Angeles.

When she returned home she spoke with Mrs. Hutchinson. "He is a gentle man but a strong teacher. He would be perfect." The leaders all talked and prayed together. They agreed that they should ask him to come.

Neely wrote to William right away: "Will you come and join us in Los Angeles. Will you come and help us here?" The church collected the money for his train fare and sent it with the letter. They were so sure that God had called this man to be with them.

When William received the letter he also felt that this was what God wanted him to do.

William spoke to Charles Parham. "I believe God is calling me to go to Los Angeles and start a work there. People around the world need to experience this Pentecost and I think God wants me to take it there."

"I don't know William. You haven't been baptized in the Holy Spirit yet, you can't speak in tongues. How can you carry this message there?" Charles replied.

They argued for a short while, but then Charles agreed to let him go with his blessing. After all, God wanted this message to spread around the world. This would be a good start.

William traveled across the country and arrived in Los Angeles in April 1906. This was going to be the most amazing time of his life, even if it didn't feel like it when he first arrived.

CHAPTER 4

THE SEEDS OF REVIVAL

William Seymour ready to preach

THE FIRST MEETING

When William arrived in Los Angeles the city was ready for revival. William could feel God's destiny hanging over his life and he could feel that God was hovering over the city too. So when a large group of people gathered for the first meeting William was excited.

He started teaching from Acts 2:4 *"All the people were filled with the Holy Spirit and began to speak in other tongues"* (English Standard Version).

As he spoke God seemed to carry his words home with extra strength. "You have not been baptized in the Holy Spirit unless you can speak in tongues. I can't speak in tongues yet, but this is what it says in the Bible so this is what we must ask God for."

It was such a strong message. No one could ignore what he said, but not everyone agreed with him. "This man is crazy," some said. "No, he's not," others replied. "We want to hear him some more."

Brother Lee invited William to come and have lunch with his family. As William left he did not realize how his teaching had divided the mission.

When William came back for the evening meeting Mrs. Hutchinson was already there. She had closed the doors and locked them with a padlock. "You are a trouble maker. This nonsense about tongues will not be preached in my mission. You are not allowed to be involved in any activities here. Now go away."

Mrs. Hutchinson had been kicked out from the Baptist church for preaching a radical message. Now she was kicking William out because his message was too radical for her!

LET'S SEEK GOD

William was devastated. He had traveled all this way to do God's work. He believed God had told him to come. They had paid for his train fare to get there and had given him a room in the mission. Now, before he had really started, he had been kicked out of the mission, banned from the bed they had given him to sleep in and left without any money to get home again.

How could things have gone so wrong? What was God doing?

Brother Lee felt he had no choice but to ask William to stay with them for a while. He didn't agree with what William had taught but he couldn't see a fellow Christian kicked out onto the streets. "After all, Jesus wants us to look after visitors, not throw them out," he explained to his wife.

William spent days in his room praying and fasting. He cried out to God trying to work out what he was doing there and what God wanted him to do next. God was about to move he could tell. But what was his part in it all.

For years William had been praying for 7 hours a day, desperate for God to work through him. Now the more he prayed the more he found himself praying for revival to come to Los Angeles. He prayed less for himself and more for the city.

After several days William invited the Lee family to join him in prayer. They started to pray with him and as they prayed God changed something in their heart. God was about to do something.

The more Lee prayed with William the more he wanted to pray when he was alone. He didn't believe in the message of Pentecost and he thought all the stories of people shaking were strange, but he really wanted more of God.

THE FIRST SIGNS OF PENTECOST

Other people from the mission saw that Lee was becoming hungrier for God. People started to join William and Lee as they prayed together.

Then one day, when Lee was praying, he had a vision. In the vision he saw Peter and John from the Bible. The two men lifted their hands to Heaven to pray. When they prayed they began to shake and speak in tongues. As Lee watched the vision, his whole body started to shake as well!

He was frightened by the whole experience. God had touched him in a totally new way and he did not expect it. He now understood what William had been talking about.

"William," Lee said one night, "I want you to lay hands on me and ask God to fill me with the Holy Spirit."

William hesitated. He knew that God said not to lay hands on people suddenly, so he just carried on praying. As they prayed some more William knew God wanted him to do it.

"Brother, I lay my hands on you in Jesus name."

As William put his hands on Lee's head, Lee fell onto the floor.

"What have you done? You've killed him. You've killed my husband." His wife cried out.

William could see how scared they were. They were not scared of God, they were just scared because they didn't understand what was happening. William knew that they would have to wait a bit longer.

"Lord, please help Lee get up again," he prayed.

A few minutes later Lee sat up. He knew he had been touched by God and would never be the same again. He prayed day and night, whenever he could.

YOUR PROBLEM IS WITH GOD, NOT ME

Meanwhile Mrs. Hutchinson was annoyed. People were leaving her church to go and pray with William. William was still preaching about tongues, something that she did not believe in. She met with other leaders of the Holiness movement and they decided to speak to William.

The leaders were not kind to William and tried to show him he was wrong. But William had a Bible in his hand. He opened it up to Acts 2:4 and read out loud:

"All the people were filled with the Holy Spirit and began to speak in other tongues."

"You have a problem with what I am teaching. But you need to know something: your problem is not with me. It is with the Word of God. Unless you have had the same experience that they had in Acts at Pentecost in that upper room, you have not been baptized in the Holy Spirit."

The leaders could not answer him.

MOVE TO BONNIE BRAE

Back in Lee's house the prayer meeting continued to grow. His house was now too small to hold everyone who was coming. Lee's friend, Richard Asbury, invited William to come and stay with them.

Mr. Asbury lived with his wife and family in a large house. As people met together to pray, their house was turned into a church every night.

William could see how hungry people were, but something bothered him. Nobody had received the gift of tongues yet. He hadn't received it either, so he wrote to Charles Parham back in Texas. "Charles, can you send some people here to help? I want people here to be baptized in the Holy Spirit."

William's wish was about to come true.

CHAPTER 5

THE ARRIVAL OF REVIVAL

The Asbury home in Bonnie Brae Street

BREAKOUT OF TONGUES

One evening at supper, Lee asked William to pray for him again. As William prayed, Lee started to speak in other tongues. That night in the prayer meeting the service began as usual. People sang some songs to God and shared testimonies.

William opened his Bible at Acts 2:4 and preached from it again. When he finished speaking, Lee lifted his hands up to Heaven and started to speak in the heavenly language of tongues.

Jennie Moore was sitting nearby. As Lee spoke she fell off her stool on to the floor. When she opened her mouth to speak she found herself speaking in tongues. That night she spoke in six different languages as the Holy Spirit worked through her. After each language it was translated into English.

Then Jennie got up and went over to the piano. She had never played a piano in her life, but she played it beautifully and sang in the Spirit at the same time. God had not only given her the gift of speaking in the special prayer language called tongues, He had also taught her to play the piano too!

Other people fell to the floor or found themselves speaking in tongues. Children who were there were baptized in the Holy Spirit. It was all very noisy as God touched different people.

Richard Asbury's daughter came running in from the kitchen to find out what was happening. When she saw the crowd she was amazed. People ran out of the house into the yard, still speaking in tongues and praising God. They wanted the whole world to know what was happening.

God had found a group of people who were not trying to grow their own ministry, but who were simply seeking Him. They weren't proud and God had chosen to show himself to them.

And so it was on April 9, 1906 that Pentecost came to Los Angeles.

THE REST OF THE WEEK

The next day people came to the house. They had heard what had happened the night before and wanted to be a part of it. Black people and white people came together to meet God. The crowds were so big that not everybody could get inside.

A lot of those who did manage to get inside fell to the ground as God's power filled them.

For the next three days meetings took place in the house day and night. There were so many people there that the whole yard was full. The porch became the pulpit and the street became the pews.

The more people came, the more God seemed to pour out His Spirit. Soon people were falling down to the ground even when they got near to the house. The power of God was so strong around that place.

Imagine if that happened in your house, in your street. What do you think your neighbors would make of it? It would certainly get them talking about God, wouldn't it. And that's exactly what happened in Bonnie Brae Street.

Over the next few days hundreds of people were saved and many people were healed. At times the whole house seemed to shake. It was just like in the days of the Book of Acts.

On the third day William stayed late praying with a friend. He was desperate to be baptized in the Holy Spirit and speak in tongues. "Maybe it's not the right time for you," his friend said.

But William refused to give up. "The right time is NOW."

A short time later he felt a mass of white-hot fire falling on him. He knew it was God and was unable to stand. Then he found himself praying in tongues. They had prayed until 4 o'clock in the morning and God had heard their prayer.

IT SPREADS

Jennie Moore had been the first woman to speak in tongues in Los Angeles. That experience changed her life. When she went to work on Friday she spoke in tongues in front of her bosses. They were so shocked that they gave her a week off work so that she could rest and "get back to normal."

Meanwhile Cena Osterberg was praying for a lady with a broken leg to be healed. When one of the intercessors from the Bonnie Brae meetings heard her praying she went to join her in prayer. Afterwards the lady invited Cena and her husband to come to the meeting.

But Cena's husband wasn't interested in going. He had been working hard all day and was tired. Cena did not want to miss out on God's blessing. So Cena went by herself. Cena could feel God's presence there and could not wait to tell others about it.

The next evening she went to her church. Her son was the pastor and with his permission she shared what had happened.

Cena's son and some of the men from his church decided to go and see what was happening. As they came near to the house they heard the singing. There was a general sigh of relief. "These people are singing like we do. It can't be that weird."

But as soon as they got into the building they were in for a shock: black people and white people were worshiping God together.

"What is this place?" Cena's son wondered. "What kind of mess are we walking into?"

But he did not have to wonder for long. As he heard people sharing their testimonies and singing in tongues he knew it was a holy place. When people prayed their faces looked like angels. Nobody was forcing them to pray, nobody was laying their hands on them. Nobody was hyping them up to make them excited. These people were simply being so touched by God that they could not hold it in any more.

Cena's son had arrived thinking he was an expert leader in God's church. Before long he realized that he needed more of God too.

Afterwards he told his mom, "I realized that I had to get humble or else I wasn't going to get very far with God there."

SHOULD WE MOVE?

All across the city people were hearing what God was doing at 214 Bonnie Brae Street.

The meetings were loud, full and often went on through the night. Some of the neighbors were starting to complain. They did not like the crowds who were passing by their houses and falling to the ground. The late night meetings were fine for a couple of days but the noise was too much for them to put up with forever.

It was also clear that the large house in Bonnie Brae Street was not going to be big enough. So the search began for a new place.

Nobody could have predicted that this was only the beginning of the most major move of God that century. God was about to do something so extraordinary, something so supernatural that it would change the Church around the world.

AZUSA STREET

Sign to Azusa Street

A STABLE

312 Azusa Street was an old, rundown building in the middle of an industrial area. There were not too many houses around, which meant there were not many neighbors who could be disturbed.

The building had been an African Methodist Church. By 1903 so many people had moved away as the factories had opened up, that the congregation left the building to find somewhere nearer to people's homes.

The building had then been turned into apartments, but a fire had destroyed part of the building. The pitched roof had been changed into a flat roof and by 1906 it was being used as a stable to store hay and cattle.

It was very basic and very rundown. The ceiling was low, the walls had not been finished properly and you could still see where the fire had destroyed part of the building. There was no plumbing inside and only one toilet outside.

When William walked in, there was dirt on the floor, straw mats scattered around and cobwebs in every possible corner.

It was certainly a very humble building. But then Jesus isn't bothered about buildings, He is concerned about people knowing Him. He loves people and wants them to follow Him. That's why when Jesus first came to Earth, He wasn't born in a posh palace but in a humble stable.

Nobody would be coming to enjoy the luxury of the building that was for sure. It was only really fit for animals to meet in, but God knew it was the perfect place.

William thought it would be perfect too, if he could pay the rent. It was only $8 a month, but he did not have the money.

GOD PROVIDES

One night William was praying to God, "God please show me how I can pay for that building."

God spoke to William, "When this service ends get on a tram and go to Pasadena."

William didn't question God, but as soon as the service ended he got on a tram. At 10:30 p.m. that evening God led him to the door of a house.

The white lady who answered the door was shocked to see a half-blind, bearded black man standing on her doorstep. She was even more surprised when he told her, "You're praying for revival, right?"

"Yes."

"I am the man God has sent to preach in the revival."

The lady invited him in and introduced him to all the people in her house. They had all met together to pray for revival and had been doing so for weeks. They were amazed at God's answer to their prayers.

William preached to them and after he had preached they gave him enough money to rent the warehouse in Azusa Street.

LET'S GET IT READY

A group of people worked to get the place ready. A pulpit was made out of two wooden shoe boxes, covered in cotton. There was no platform for the pulpit to stand on. It was probably only worth 15 cents. But it did what it needed to do.

A group of laborers came in to clean the building, paint the walls and fix the windows. They brought some wooden barrels in and nailed planks across them to make benches for people to sit on.

A Roman Catholic even built an altar for free so that people could kneel before God there.

The upstairs room was turned into a place for the workers to live in and an upper room. This upper room was set aside for people to wait for the Holy Spirit to come, just like the disciples in Acts had waited for the Holy Spirit in an upper room. A big sign was put up in the room, "no talking above a whisper." The people wanted to make sure that nobody was disturbed when seeking God there.

The people worked hard and fast to transform the building. When they had finished it was still very basic, but at least it was clean and safe.

THE FIRST EASTER

The first service was held on Easter Saturday, April 14, 1906. Around 15 people met together during the day to seek God there. For the next few nights the meetings carried on in Bonnie Brae Street too.

But God was preparing to move in Azusa Street.

Back in Pastor Smale's church, on Easter Sunday, Jennie Moore stood up to tell people what had happened. Pastor Smale had been to the revival in Wales and so knew that when God moved nobody could make it happen.

He was very interested to hear what she had to say. But he was even more interested in what happened after she had spoken.

Jennie told them all about the prayer meetings and how people were being baptized in the Holy Spirit. Then she spoke in tongues.

When she had finished someone translated what she said. *"This is what God spoke about through the prophet Joel. I will pour out my spirit on all people ..."* (See Joel 2:28-29.).

Other people in the congregation started to speak in tongues. Some people shouted out praise to God. Others ran out onto the street. They were not ready to be this close to God. People stood talking about this move of God.

More people got involved in the Azusa Street meetings. Time after time people came away from the meetings saying, "I have never experienced anything like it in my life."

IN THE PAPERS

On Tuesday, April 17, The Los Angeles Daily times sent a reporter to the mission. "These people are crazy. The meetings are crazy. People babble on in this weird language they call tongues. The whole thing is strange. It is mainly black people, but there are a few white people there too."

The report was not very positive. But it didn't need to be because God was working to make things happen. The next morning, as the papers were being printed, nearby San Francisco was being shaken by a huge earthquake.

Around noon the earthquake reached Los Angeles shaking the city twice. People panicked as the earthquake struck.

They remembered how small they were and began to see that there was something bigger than them. They were not in control of the world, somebody else was. This was just what people needed to shake them into thinking about their lives.

San Francisco had been completely destroyed. Hundreds of people had died and loads of buildings had been damaged. Hundreds of millions of dollars were needed to repair the buildings (nowadays the price tag would be billions of dollars!)

One newspaper had a cartoon in it showing the grim reaper standing over San Francisco. The message was clear— life does not go on forever.

People remembered the gap in their lives that they had tried to ignore: the gap which God wanted to fill. God was shouting to try and get people's attention. And people were starting to open their hearts to God.

Frank Bartleman wrote a tract telling people to turn back to God. Within weeks 40,000 copies had been given out in Los Angeles and the tract had also been given elsewhere.

All the preparation work had now taken place. People were ready to meet with God and God was definitely ready to meet with them.

CHAPTER 7

THE GLORY DESCENDS

William Seymour standing outside the building in 312 Azusa Street

THE GOD OF ALL PEOPLE

Los Angeles had always been very tolerant of different races. People from all over the world lived in there, but they did not mix together. Overnight God broke down barriers that had stopped people of different races coming together.

Thirty days after the earthquake it seemed like people from every nation were coming together in Azusa Street to meet with God.

A few months after Azusa Street had opened the place was packed beyond capacity. Every space was filled as 800 people squeezed into the building. It was difficult to breathe and impossible to move around because of the number of people there.

Another 500 people would stand outside the building trying to get in. They struggled to see what was going on inside, but if they listened carefully they could hear the meeting. They wanted to stand on the street and be near God rather than sit at home missing out.

SKEPTICS CONVERTED

As stories started to spread a lot of people thought it was very strange. They had not been to any of the meetings at Azusa Street but they had heard of people shaking, speaking in strange languages and acting weird.

Those who actually bothered to go and find out about it were amazed. They could feel God's presence. Many of the skeptics became supporters after just one visit. People who went to Azusa Street realized that this really was God at work.

Often, when proud people walked into the building, they would stop. For a moment they would lose their breath and be unable to go on. The congregation would pray for them and God would work in their hearts so that they would see their need of Him.

I UNDERSTAND NOW

One missionary traveled all the way from the Philippines to come and prove that tongues was nonsense. He wanted the people to know that they were being tricked. As he approached the building he could feel himself getting angrier as he thought about what he had heard.

The congregation noticed that the man was not right with God and started to pray for him. This made him even more angry. He couldn't wait for the preacher to start so that he could give him a piece of his mind.

As he stood there a woman came up to him and spoke in tongues. The man was numbed into shock. The lady was actually speaking a rare language from one of the tribes he had worked with in the Philippines. There was no way anyone there could know that language.

But this lady was speaking it!

Suddenly he realized that they were not the ones who were wrong—he was! God had brought him all the way from the Philippines to show him.

As the man knelt at the wooden plank that was the altar, he started to cry out to God. He repented because of his attitude. Another lady came to him and started to speak in tongues. Again the man understood the language. This time it was a language from one of the more friendly tribes in the Philippines.

He understood every word. She said: "This is the thing that happened in Acts 2. You will receive power when the Holy Spirit comes on you."

The man wept at the altar—"Lord baptize me in your Holy Spirit." The people around him prayed and before long he was speaking in tongues!

OTHER LANGUAGES

Another time a lady spoke perfectly in German even though she had never learned the language. Two German speakers were in separate parts of the building. When they heard her speaking they translated what she said so that those around them could understand it.

Afterwards they found that both of the translators had said the same words—it really was German and they really had translated what she said—they weren't making it up.

One woman was praying when God knocked her to the ground. For the next three days she saw visions of Heaven and hell. When she got up she spoke in tongues. A minister recognized that she was actually speaking Hebrew (the language that the Old Testament was originally written in). When he translated what she said he realized she had just said Psalm 23.

But the main thing that marked out the meetings was not the gift of tongues. It was the presence of God.

THE SHEKINAH GLORY

Meetings ran into each other as people did not want to go home, or even pause to eat. They just wanted to be in God's presence. For three years there were three services a day, seven days a week.

Services sometimes ran through the night until the next morning when more people would arrive for the first service of the next day.

All this time God's presence was there.

God's presence was so powerful that people tried to find a word to describe it. In the days of Moses, God's presence used to live the tabernacle. It was like a cloud. The Jews called it 'the Shekinah Glory' of God. When the glory moved on the people moved on with it.

It was a sign of God's presence living with the Jews.

In Azusa Street people realized that God had chosen to come and hover over that place. The building was basic, but God was there.

Often a cloud filled the building. The people who went to Azusa called it the Shekinah Glory of God.

A prophetess called Jean Darnell told the story of a three year old child who was in Azusa Street. She used to sleep under one of the benches as the cloud filled the room. She would wake up to see this thick mist in the room and try to capture it in her arms. It was when she grew up that she realized she was touching the glory of God.

People started to notice that when the greatest miracles took place the mist of God's glory grew thicker. You couldn't blow it away with a fan, but you could walk through it. At times it even seemed to be glowing with light.

When you were in the mist it felt like you were breathing in pure oxygen. It was as if life went through your whole body.

Sometimes the mist was so thick that it would fill the whole room. William had seen the mist often in the meetings, but each time he was still amazed at it. He would sit and enjoy it while the meeting continued.

People talked about the mist in hushed tones, it was like a taste of Heaven on Earth. God was visibly there. You could feel Him. With God so close it seemed like impossible things could easily happen.

And they did.

CHAPTER 8

MIRACLES

The Azusa Street ministry team

ORDINARY PEOPLE DOING EXTRAORDINARY THINGS

God had clearly called William to lead the revival. But God had not called William to do everything. God chose to use ordinary people. Men and women, black and white, young and old were all used by God.

Sister Carney was 17 years old when she started going to the church on Azusa Street. When God told William to go a house to be given money for the building in Azusa Street, she had been there praying for revival. She was there when they cleaned and prepared the building. She was there when the Shekinah Glory of God filled the building and she saw God do many miracles.

One time a woman came into the meeting with a bloody bandage on the side of her head. She was in a lot of pain. Sister Carney went over to her. "Are you okay, what's wrong?"

The lady waited a moment before she spoke. "I got into a fight with another lady and she bit my ear off."

The lady carefully took off the bandage. Sister Carney saw her head was still bleeding and there was no ear. It looked disgusting.

Sister Carney didn't want to talk any more, she just wanted to pray. "Lord, heal this ear, in Jesus name."

The lady looked up and smiled, "the pain has gone. The pain has gone completely!"

Sister Carney looked up at the wound. As she watched an ear started to form from nowhere. She continued watching as a brand new ear grew on the side of the ladies head.

THE LAME WALK

Sister Carney prayed for lots of people with all kinds of illnesses. But she really loved praying for people in wheelchairs.

Before she prayed she would move the footrests out of the way. After all if God was going to heal the person, then they would be able to stand up and if they were going to stand they would need to move them out of the way.

With God's glory living in that place, Sister Carney expected people to be healed. Time after time she watched people come in wheelchairs and walk out pushing them.

One man had heavy braces on his legs. As soon as he entered Azusa Street Sister Carney went to him. She lifted up the foot rests and put his heavy legs on the floor.

"Get up and walk," she told the man.

"But I can't walk, I am wearing these heavy braces," the man replied.

Sister Carney told some people to remove the braces so he could walk. When they removed the braces he got up and walked for the first time in years. God not only healed his legs, but made his legs strong at the same time.

EXPECT IT

The people in the Azusa Street meetings expected God to heal. Many of the young people saw at least five people healed in each meeting as they prayed for the sick. With so many people praying, hundreds were healed each day.

Many of the young people watched Sister Carney and started to talk about the Carney rule of faith:

"If you expect God to heal the person then you better get them ready for the healing: take off the braces, remove the footrests from the wheelchair."

This simple act of faith showed God that they were trusting Him and expecting Him to heal.

Ralphy Riggs was twelve years old when he saw a husband and wife come in wheelchairs, pushed by their teenage children. He went running over, "Have you come to be healed?" he asked. "Yes," they replied.

Both of them were suffering with a temperature, and too ill to move.

Ralphy started to pray. But then he stopped.

"Remember the Carney rule," he said to himself. He bent down, lifted up the footrests on the wheelchairs and then stood up and prayed.

As he prayed the lady began to shake. Soon she was standing up and running around the room. The man simply stood up and started shouting at the top of his voice: "Thank you God. Thank you God."

Ralphy had remembered the 'Carney rule' of faith. He had shown God that he expected them to be healed and God had answered his prayer of faith.

THE BLIND SEE

Many blind people were healed instantly at Azusa Street, but one lady's healing stands out.

She had been blind in both eyes from birth. The white parts in her eyes had never developed so when you looked into her eyes you would just see darkness.

She was prayed for by one of the men there. After he had prayed for her, he looked up. She opened her eyes and he saw the whiteness there for the first time. He was about to start praising God but he didn't get a chance.

When the woman opened her eyes she was so shocked to see light and people for the first time. The experience was new to her and she did not know how to cope.

"Aaaaaaaaaagh!" she screamed at the top of her voice.

Once she had calmed down enough to explain what was happening everyone started jumping around the place. They were so excited at what God had done.

THE SOUNDS OF REVIVAL

For a moment try to imagine being in Azusa Street. The building is very basic. The seats are not comfortable but you can feel and see God's presence there.

There is a strange mix of smells: perfumes and the smell of people in a hot room. There is also the faint smell of hay still hanging around the building.

And then there are the sounds you can hear.

At times there is pure heavenly worship as people sing in many different languages. At times there are hymns being sung as people of all ages and races unite together to worship God.

There is also the sound of heavenly music. As the musicians play, the music somehow lifts you closer to God. There is a violin that seems to stir something inside you as it's played. Somehow it makes you want more of God. With a choir of voices singing in a heavenly language it is as if God himself is singing out the music. The sound of the music alone is enough to bring people to Jesus.

Some of the sounds are stranger. People sobbing before God as they realize that He has forgiven them all of their sins. Shouting and clapping, stamping feet and people running around the room making nose.

These people may look a bit crazy until you realize that they have been healed from blindness, freed from death, or are walking for the first time in their life. When you know that, you understand why they are shouting.

You would do the same if you were healed of something so serious! When you see a miracle like this you want to shout praise to God, even if it didn't happen to you.

But close your eyes because there is one more sound I want you to hear. It is the sound of bones clicking and crunching together, and popping into sockets. As people were prayed for, you could hear God straightening out their bodies and fixing broken bones.

It sounds a bit like people cracking their knuckles. But it's the sound of healing. God's will being done on Earth as it was in Heaven.

Expectations were very high. Everyone there knew that nothing was impossible for God—they had seen God do incredible things. As God reigned over it all, His servant William Seymour was right in the middle of it, waiting for instructions from God.

CHAPTER 9

THE BOX

William would have worn a box similar to this on his head

A HUMBLE LEADER

William lived in the building, but he was not at every meeting. He couldn't be. The meetings ran nearly nonstop for three years and he needed to sleep sometimes!

When he was not there, the workers would start ministering to the different people, leading them to Jesus and praying for people to be healed and filled with the Holy Spirit.

William would come downstairs and sit near the homemade pulpit made from two wooden shoe boxes one placed on top of the other. He would sit at the homemade pulpit with his head inside the top box and pray, often throughout the entire meeting. He didn't even seem to move.

This was not William's revival, there was no pride there, it was God's revival. William's job was to do what God told him to do without questioning it. As it says in Romans 6:16, William was now a slave of Christ. William knew that slaves had to do what their masters told them to do.

When William put his head in the box there was a glow that appeared around it. It was just like Moses' face used to shine after he had spoken with God and like Jesus' face shone in the transfiguration. People could see that something holy was happening there.

Nobody dared touch the box, or even to go near the glow. Even when William was not there people felt that the box was sacred.

As long as William had his head in the box, people carried on the meeting, but as soon as he removed his head from the box people would look to see what God was going to do through him. They knew he had received his instructions from God.

THE UNPREDICTABLE MAN

When William removed his head from the box, anything could happen. Each time God gave him different orders to do things in different ways. Sometimes he would tell them to sing a particular song. Other times he would tell everyone to sing in the Spirit. When he did this people would start singing in the heavenly language of tongues.

Sometimes William would walk to where people sat in wheelchairs, "Everyone in wheelchairs you are healed in Jesus name." At that moment ALL of the people in the wheelchairs would stand up.

At other times he would go over to those who had been brought there from the hospitals. Some were so sick that they lay on beds unable to get up. Each one had different diseases, all were seriously ill, many were dying. "Everyone on the beds you are healed in Jesus name." At that moment, no matter what was wrong with them, ALL of the people on the beds would get up healed.

One time he pointed to where a load of people with arthritis were sitting. Their bones were all deformed and had been eaten by the disease; many of them were in pain.

"Do you want to see a miracle over there? Every one of you within a few minutes are going to be up and walking in the name of Jesus." As he finished speaking bones started to crack and pop into place as every single person in that area was healed.

COPYING WILLIAM

Ralphy, the twelve year old who prayed for many people to be healed, watched William at work. He often tried to copy him and declared that everyone was healed. But only once did God answer his prayers for this kind of mass healing.

A whole load of people arrived from an old people's home. They were all very frail. Many were suffering from arthritis and other troubles.

"Every one of you is going to be healed in the name of Jesus. Now all of you be healed."

As Ralphy stood there, he heard the sound of joints clicking and before him stood a group of elderly people, no longer frail, no longer careful in their movements. They now had the energy of their youth again.

Ralphy realized that you can't just say what you want to happen. You have to do what God tells you to do, then God moves.

SUPERNATURAL HEALINGS

Sometimes God would lead William to pray for an individual. One man who came forward had growths all over his face. He looked so ugly. When William prayed for him the growths fell off his face onto the floor. His face was left perfectly smooth.

When he went home people had to sweep up the growths from the floor.

One day a man came forward and asked for prayer. His leg had been chopped off and so he had a wooden leg in its place. But where the stump joined to the wood gangrene, caused by an infection, had started to develop.

The man was scared. He could not have the stump chopped off, but if the gangrene was not healed it could spread to his whole body and kill him.

William looked at the man. "What did you come here for?"

"I want you to pray for my stump. It is starting to get gangrene where the wooden leg attaches."

William answered him, "I'm just upset because you still have the wooden leg on. It would be a challenge for God to grow a leg out when the wooden leg is attached."

The man took the wooden leg off and stood on his good leg in front of William.

William placed his hand on the man and prayed, "Let your name be glorified. In the name of Jesus, I command this leg to grow out. The gangrene is gone; you are healed."

As people watched a new leg started to grow out from the stump. This was not some special effect in a movie. This was the real thing happening right in front of their eyes. Within a few seconds he was standing on two legs.

The next moment he was running up and down. Nobody could stop him and nobody wanted to. They were too busy praising God.

William didn't bother preaching that night—God had already taught His people through that one miracle.

A year later a man came in who had lost an arm in an accident.

William reminded everybody of how God had healed the man with the gangrene on his leg before. Then he turned to the to the man with the arm missing and said:

"Can you work with just one arm?"

"I am only given badly paid jobs. I hardly have enough money to eat."

William felt sorry for him. "That's not good. Are you married?"

"Yes."

"Got kids?"

"Yes."

"This man needs to be able to make a living. This man needs to work and he needs to have enough to feed this family."

Then he slapped the man on the shoulder and spoke, "Arm grow out in Jesus name."

Almost immediately the arm grew out.

The man couldn't believe it. He was in total shock. As he moved the new arm he was speechless. He kept touching it with his other hand. In a matter of seconds God had done a completely impossible thing.

A few weeks later the man came back.

This time he brought 200 people with him. He told everyone how he had been given his old job back. Many of the people who came with him were healed and saved that night.

We follow a big God who is able to do impossible things. And He will work through anyone. All we have to do is obey Him.

CHAPTER 10

HEALINGS EVERYONE COULD SEE

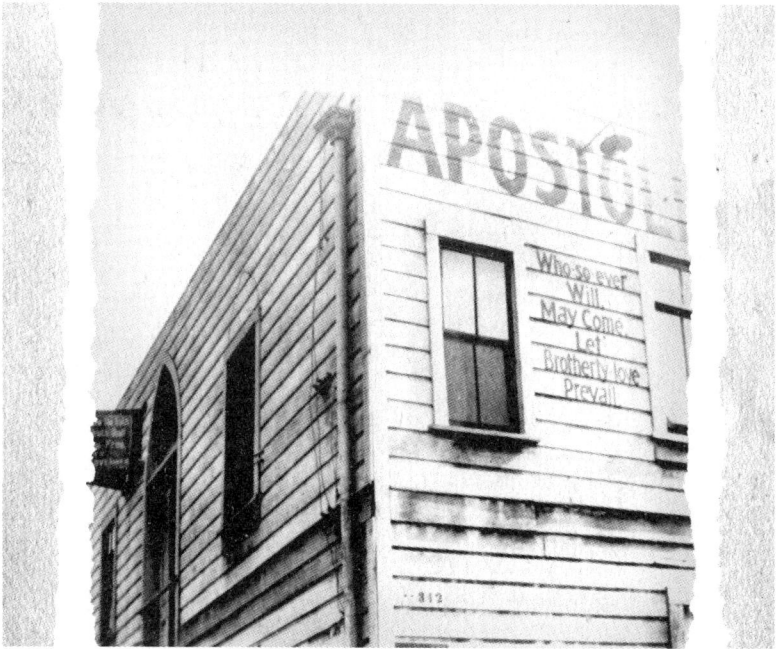

Close up of the outside of 312 Azusa Street

FINGERS GROW BACK

Many healings took place in Azusa Street, so many in fact, that people soon came there believing and expecting God to move in wondrous and miraculous ways.

One man came to the meeting with only three fingers on one hand. He had lost the other two in an accident a few weeks before.

He was greeted by one of the workers, "Let's see what God can do,"

"What do you mean?" The man replied.

"Let's see if God can grow you some new fingers." And with that the worker prayed.

As he prayed the fingers started to grow. One lady was so amazed that she fainted.

The man just stared at his hand. He could not believe what had just happened, but he also couldn't deny it. The worker then took him around the people to show them what God had done saying:

"Look, this man did not have two of his fingers. Now they are all there."

As the people looked they saw that even his new fingers had fully grown fingernails on them.

HUNCHBACK HEALED

One lady was a hunchback. Twenty years before, when she was around thirty years old, she started to get problems in her back. Bit by bit her back had become more twisted until she could hardly move. The doctors wanted to put her in a nursing home, but she refused to go.

When she was prayed for there was a loud cracking sound and her back started to separate and click back into place. Within minutes she was totally healed, running around the room and praising God.

LEGS UNTWIST

Another man had come in a wheelchair. Two years before his legs had been run over by a train. Doctors had told him that they wanted to cut off his legs. They had been broken in many places and were so twisted that there was no hope of them ever getting better.

But in Azusa Street there was always hope, because God was there.

One man started to pray for him, but he was stopped by Sister Carney.

"Hold on a minute, if he is going to be healed we need to do something first." She bent down and moved the footrests of the wheelchair out of the way.

"Now we can pray."

As they prayed together, they heard a loud cracking sound and saw the man's legs untwist. Before long his legs were completely straight. Then he stood to his feet and started running about. And everyone who had seen the miracle was running around with him.

LOADS MORE MIRACLES

Some people came with cleft palates—they had a gap in their gum. Not only was there no teeth in the middle at the top of their mouth, but there was no gum and no lip either. After prayer the gap closed up perfectly and new teeth grew.

People with one leg shorter than the other were amazed as they watched a leg grow. Kidney stones that were causing pain simply vanished after prayer.

A man with a tumor on his spine was due to have an X-ray the next day. You could see the lump through his shirt. When he was prayed for the lump disappeared. On the X-ray there was no sign of the tumor.

One lady came with a broken wrist. It had been crushed when it was hit with a hammer. After prayer it was totally healed.

Many teeth were fixed. Teeth that had fallen out grew back, crooked teeth straightened up and when teeth had holes in them gunk would pour out onto a handkerchief as God healed them. One man had rotten teeth and red gums. They were so bad that an infection had even spread to his face. After a couple of rounds of prayer he was completely healed. In fact he never had any more problems with his teeth for the rest of his life.

A multitude of miracles took place, every day. Children and young teens were running around having a great time praying for the sick and watching them get healed. They would walk right over to the people as they came in and pray for them. Each night the young people would see miracle after miracle take place.

People who couldn't hear and those who couldn't speak were healed. One time 35 deaf people stood in a circle holding hands. Every single one of them was healed after prayer.

One lady went to the meetings for two years. In that time she prayed for over 3000 tumors to be healed. And they were. God was healing many people of many different kinds of diseases.

And wherever God was working, the children wanted to be a part of it. One boy was too small to see what God was doing, so he would stand on a bench to watch the miracles. He did not want to miss out on anything.

CHILDREN HEALED

A little girl came to the meeting. When she was two she started to go blind and by the age of four she could see nothing. She was now six years old and her eyes were grey. She had suffered for years already, but in a few seconds she was completely healed by God.

A young boy stood near the pulpit. He had crutches to help him walk because his legs were badly crippled. One man came over to him. "Why is no one praying for you?"

The boy just shrugged his shoulders.

"Would you like to be healed?" the man asked.

The boy nodded his head.

So the man took the crutches from him and prayed. At first the boy didn't feel anything, but then he felt electricity running through his legs. He could actually move them.

"I'm healed, I'm healed," the boy cried.

A young girl was also crippled. She was only eight years old, but her legs were in braces and she needed crutches to walk. Someone prayed for her but nothing happened.

Then a lady came over. "Would you like Jesus to heal you."

"Oh, yes," the girl replied.

The lady knew the Carnie rule, so she took the girls braces off and took the crutches from the girl.

"Right you are going to have to be healed now."

The girl started to cry. She really wanted to be healed but she was not sure if Jesus would do it for her.

"Let's pray," the lady said. After she prayed, she told the girl to stand.

"But I can't."

"Oh, you can. You just need to try."

Very carefully the girl tried to stand. She was amazed that she could. She started to stamp her feet and found her legs were suddenly strong again. That girl danced and ran around for hours.

God healed a six year old boy who could not walk. He was strapped into his wheelchair because he could not even hold his head up by himself. Before they prayed they unstrapped him. Minutes later the boy wanted to get down to play.

EVEN THE BABIES

A baby accidently swallowed someone's strong medicines at home. By the time the mom arrived at the mission the child had stopped breathing and was cold. The baby had died. But the mom cried out to God to heal her child and the baby came back to life.

Another mom brought her baby to the meeting. The child was under a year old, but could not make any sound. The baby's neck was bent over and the mom knew the baby was in pain, even though the baby couldn't cry.

One of the workers picked up the baby and put a blanket over the child's head so that the mom could not see her baby. Then she started to pray.

As she was praying and holding the baby, she could feel the child's neck moving. The worker was so excited she wanted to jump around, but she had to be careful because she was still holding the young child. So the worker looked at the baby and started to cry, God had totally healed the child.

"Why are you crying? What's wrong with my baby?" the mom asked.

The lady pulled back the blanket so the mother could see what had happened. When the mom saw it she was filled with excitement and joy and ran all over the room shouting what God had done.

Back at home the father was amazed at what had happened to his child. He went to the next meeting, and was saved. He later became a pastor of one of the largest churches in Los Angeles.

God really does want every single person to be well.

CHAPTER 11

GOD CARES ABOUT PEOPLE

William Seymour—a gentle leader

BODY, SOUL AND SPIRIT

God loves making people well. But even more than that He loves it when people choose to leave their sin and follow Him. God loves people so much He wants them to be whole in their body, soul and spirit, even if they don't believe in Him.

So when a homeless alcoholic walked into the room, the people of Azusa Street could feel just how much God loved the man. Normally people would ignore a drunken man, but God never ignores people who come to Him for help.

God spoke to one of the workers, "go and pray for him." At first they weren't so sure, but they knew they had to obey God.

As they moved closer to the man they could smell the alcohol on him. Moving closer still they noticed something else, "You're blind!"

"That's why I came here," the man said. He was slurring his words because of the alcohol. "I want to be healed."

The worker prayed for the man and God healed him immediately. He could see, he didn't want to drink alcohol anymore. Even the smell of alcohol had disappeared from him! It was like God had given him a bath to take the smell away!

This man didn't go running around. He just sat and wept. Finally he spoke, "well, it's true. I've been healed." He was amazed that God would care about someone like him who had wasted his life. God cares about everybody.

For the rest of his life he travelled around telling people what Jesus had done for him. God had chosen him, even if nobody else would have.

PLASTIC SURGERY

God cares about what we care about. One lady walked in and she had no nose. Cancer had eaten it all away. One of the workers prayed for her, but nothing happened.

"Sometimes God heals straight away, other times he does it over time," the worker explained.

The next day the lady came back and her nose was perfect.

I guess if you were in the Azusa Street meetings you would have expected God to heal that lady. After all it was cancer. It would have continued to eat away at her face. When God healed another lady's nose it was even more surprising.

The lady had a hook on the end of her nose. It wasn't a disease; it just looked a bit funny. She had thought of going to a doctor to get surgery but she heard God speaking to her, "I am a better doctor than any of the doctors here on Earth." So she went to Azusa Street to see what God would do.

When she was prayed for the strange hook disappeared. She looked in the mirror to see what God had done, but she still wasn't happy. "My nose still looks a bit pointy."

The worker prayed again and by the end of the meeting God had given her a perfect nose.

GOD MEETS THE DOUBTERS

One man had a horrible cancer in his throat. His neck had turned black and he couldn't talk because of the cancer. The worker put his hand on the man's neck and prayed.

But nothing happened.

"Do you believe God can heal you?" the worker asked.

The man nodded in reply.

"Are you sure?" Again the man nodded his reply.

The worker prayed and this time when he took his hands away the lump had gone and the neck was returning to a normal color.

"Now talk!" he ordered.

The man looked at him in surprise. "But I can't," he said.

"Say that again."

"I ca…" the man stopped and realized that he was talking. Even though he thought he couldn't speak, Jesus had healed him.

GOD DOES A COMPLETE JOB

When a lady came in suffering from lung cancer everyone could see she was very sick. She was so thin that you could see her bones. She pointed to one of the workers: "that's the woman I want to pray for me."

"What's the matter?" the lady asked.

"I have lung cancer. I've been losing weight for a year and now I can hardly breathe. If God does not heal me tonight I will be dead by tomorrow. Doctors say that I will probably not even live through the night.

The worker laid hands on her and prayed for her. Immediately the lady could breathe and all the pain had gone.

But it didn't stop there.

The next day the lady went to see her doctor. Her doctor thought she was a new patient. He didn't even recognize her.

When she said who she was the doctor could not believe it. "There is no way you can be better and you have put on weight. Even if you were healed you could not put on that much weight so quickly. It's impossible."

"I know I couldn't, but God could!" God had not only taken away her cancer he had given her back the weight that she had lost.

"Have you been going to that warehouse on Azusa Street?" the doctor asked.

When the lady told him what had happened the doctor

started to go to Azusa Street with her. After a few weeks he had given up medicine and spent his time praying for God to heal the sick. He even started a ministry called Wings of Healing that is still ministering today.

PERFECT HARMONY

All through Azusa Street God was doing something special. The people there were united around God. For most of his life William Seymour had been hated because he was black.

Now he was in a place where people didn't care what color you were. They just cared about whether or not you knew God. William could have chosen to hate the white people, but he didn't. Instead he chose to show them God's love.

The rich and the poor rubbed shoulders together. Professional people and uneducated people knelt to pray together. Everybody was equal before God. Night after night rich, white, well-educated people would come to hear the poor, black, uneducated, one-eyed preacher. But nobody who was there thought that was strange. God had united them together.

William was very clear. He wanted people to meet with God. Tongues was not the most important thing, even the healings were not the most important thing. Salvation was the most important.

"Don't talk about tongues ..." he would tell them, "... get people saved!" And many, many people were saved.

Several drug addicts who came, were both set free and saved at the same time. One man had been locked up in an asylum for crazy people. He used to tell people that Jesus did not exist. When he came, God met him and he spent the rest of his life telling people about Jesus.

When a burglar walked by he did not expect God to take something from him. He planned to rob some houses but was drawn into the building. Falling at the altar he left his skeleton keys there. One encounter with God had totally changed his heart. God took away his sins and he was baptized in the Holy Spirit.

Just as Jesus had healed, saved and delivered people, the same thing happened at Azusa. One man started barking like a dog and was writhing around on the floor. William told the demon to come out of him. The man became calm and was filled with the Holy Spirit.

Thousands of people were saved as God healed them and their relatives. Each new convert brought more people. The crowds kept coming and God kept meeting them. It was an awesome time.

CHAPTER 12

THE FIRE OF GOD

William Seymour with other leaders of the early Pentecostal movement. Front row: William Seymour and John Lake. 2nd row: ?, F.F. Bosworth, Tom Hezmalhalch.

FIRE!

You could feel God's presence in Azusa Street. As God did more and more amazing miracles His presence became stronger.

People got used to this cloud of God's glory. It was just like the cloud that used to be with Israelites when Moses led them in the desert. There was a cloud in the day and a pillar of fire at night.

The people of Azusa Street knew when it grew thick that God was going to do even more incredible things. They soon found out that at times when the cloud was thickest inside the building, God was also there as a fire outside on the roof.

Several times people passed by the building and saw flames coming out the top. Each time they called the fire brigade.

"But nothing is burning," the fire brigade would say when they came. "We can't see anything burning and we can't smell any smoke. There is nothing for us to do."

They could see the fire, but the building was not burning. (Just like the burning bush Moses saw in Exodus 3:2.)

One time Sister Carney went outside to see the fire for herself. As she walked away from the building she looked back and could see flames leaping from the building. They seemed to join with other flames that were leaping down from Heaven. It was a whole pillar of fire sitting on the roof.

The flames weren't always there, but when they were you could be sure that God's presence would be really strong inside the building.

DANGER ZONE

As people walked towards 312 Azusa Street they could feel something different. Even a couple of blocks away the Christians could feel God's presence. Walking along they would have to stop and pray for strength to be able to go on.

The unbelievers felt God's conviction. On some days you could walk along the streets around Azusa Street and see men and women kneeling down, crying out to God for forgiveness. Some people were even being healed on their way to the meetings.

It was like God had drawn a circle around Azusa Street. Anyone who stepped into that circle would meet with God.

As people heard what God was doing they started to travel from far away to be a part of it. One day the Azusa Street anointing spilled out further. Half a mile away in Grand Circle Station people stepped off the train. Many of them had traveled from far and planned to go to the Azusa Street meetings to meet with God.

They did not expect to meet Him in the train station. But they did!

Throughout the day people were stepping off the train and falling over. They were not tripping, they were just experiencing God's presence so strongly that they could not keep standing!

Many of them started to speak in tongues while they lay there.

People who hadn't even heard what God was doing in Azusa Street felt drawn to go to Los Angeles. When they got there God led them to the warehouse.

For those who made it as far as Azusa Street there was even more of God's glory waiting for them.

A HUMBLE MAN

Right in the center of God's glory sat a man of great prayer. He was humble. He loved God. He loved people. He was William Seymour.

William knew that he was not the only one God could use. He knew God could work through anyone.

When William preached his messages were short and full of fire. He never put people down, but everything he said seemed to be filled with God's love, even when he was correcting people for things they had done wrong. He didn't shout or wave his hands about. He just spoke slowly and clearly. But God anointed his words.

Anyone who saw him could tell that he was a man of authority. God was with him. He didn't have to force people to respond to God, they came to God because God was there. William didn't have to work anything up. He just had to pray and obey God.

William didn't put out any big advertising.

He didn't even try to control the meeting. He spent time praying instead. He had no real organization and he didn't even take up an offering. As he walked along people would put money into his pockets without him even knowing. God made sure that those who ministered had everything they needed to do the work.

For as long as William was willing to keep putting his head in the box, God was willing to work through this humble vessel. The lack of structure meant that William had to stay fully dependent on God. Even though thousands of people were going through the building somehow it all worked out without huge amounts of man's organization.

Not everything was perfect. Many people wanted to close down the meetings, but these people soon found themselves going against God.

CHAPTER 13

OPPOSITION

The Azusa Street Mission

THE PRESS

With so many people being healed and meeting God, the newspapers could not ignore what was happening in Azusa Street. But they could try to stop it.

The papers often wrote about the work of the mission. They described the people as if they were all crazy.

One paper summed it up like this:

"The people seem to be under a spell. They cry and jump and shake all through the night. All kinds of races are mixing together. It is horrible. And their leader is a one-eyed black man who can hardly read! He doesn't really do anything either. He just sits with a box on his head. Occasionally he tells people to repent."

Some of the reports just became silly. One paper wrote:

"There is a rumor that these people are planning on killing children to please their God."

Of course the people in Azusa Street would never dream of doing that.

But even though the newspapers wrote these things, God used it. As people read these stories they became interested and wanted to know what was actually happening there. Satan was trying to use the newspapers to stop the work. Instead more people ended up going to find out what was happening! The papers were giving free advertising to Azusa Street without even realizing it!

Reporters were sent to Azusa to find out more facts. The reporters came looking for horrible things to say, but some of them were surprised by what they saw.

When one reporter sat in a meeting he suddenly realized that God was really there. A lady was standing up the front, speaking in tongues. His fellow reporters had mocked these strange babbling sounds that these Christians made.

But he couldn't do it because he knew she wasn't making it up.

She was speaking in the language of the country he had been born in. As she spoke, she looked directly at the reporter. She told him about all of his sins in great detail in a language that only he could understand.

At the end of the meeting he spoke to the lady. "Did you know what you were saying?"

"Not a word," the lady replied.

That day the reporter gave his life to Jesus. Going back to work he spoke to his boss. "I cannot write what you want me to write. I can write how great it is there, but I cannot mock these people. Do you want me to write a more positive article?"

The boss took one look at him and kicked him out of the office. The reporter lost his job, but he had found something more precious. He had found Jesus.

THE PEOPLE

Owen Lee was a rough man. He was born in Ireland, but had lived in Los Angeles for a while. He was always getting into fights. One day he saw some policemen beating a drunk man. He went over to the four police officers and beat them up instead!

But when he went to Azusa Street he met Jesus and something changed inside him. All the anger disappeared. All the hate went. Instead he wanted to love people like Jesus did.

Owen Lee was about to discover that not everyone liked the Christians. When people heard how he had changed they wanted to stop him from talking about Jesus. They decided the only way they could do this was to kill him.

A tall, large-sized man approached him with a thick rope. He planned to use the rope to hang Owen. First he spat in Owen's face. Then he punched him. But Owen didn't fight back. Instead he turned the other cheek, just like Jesus tells us to.

The man lifted his fist to punch Owen again. But this time his fist was stopped in midair. The power of God had stopped it. That same invisible power then picked the man up and threw him in the gutter. Owen had done nothing. He stood watching as the man ran away in fear.

For the next few days Owen prayed for his enemies. After all God tells us to love our enemies and to pray for those who persecute us. He was so happy and knew God had answered his prayers when a few nights later he saw his enemies walking into Azusa Street and giving their lives to Jesus.

Of course not all the Azusa Street people saw God move in this way. Many of them had to put up with being cursed and abused as they walked down the streets. Some of them were rejected by their friends and their family. But they knew that God was giving them far more than they had lost, and could ever hope to receive from anyone else.

Sometimes God takes away persecution. Other times He helps us to go through it. Jesus promised us that we would be persecuted if we follow Him. But he also promised us that he would always be with us.

Many in Azusa Street said, "We are not only ready to go to prison for Jesus, we are ready to die for Him." These weren't empty words, they really meant it. A lot of them had a chance to show that they did.

THE POLICE

The police did not like what was happening in Azusa Street. If someone complained they would go there at once.

They really wanted to close down the meetings, but to do that they needed the neighbors to complain. As they knocked on the doors and spoke to the neighbors they desperately tried to find people who would complain about the noise.

But nobody did!

They could not close down the meetings so they started to arrest some of the people who went there instead. But God was still with His people.

A man was arrested and he was taken to court. As he stood in the court one of the witnesses suddenly cried out. They could see an angel standing next to him.

A couple was arrested for preaching in the streets. As they were on their way to jail they sang praise songs to God. When the police locked them away they carried on singing and praying to God at the top of the voices, just like Peter had done in the book of Acts.

After a while the police couldn't wait to let them out of jail because of all the godly noise they were making.

CRAZY TONGUES

One man was speaking in tongues when two police officers heard him. They were sure he must be crazy and so they decided to lock him up. As they traveled with him he carried on speaking in tongues. When they took him to the hospital he continued speaking in tongues. Even on his way to court he spoke in tongues.

Finally the judge arrived, and the man still kept speaking in tongues. Several people had come to be a witness for the man. But the judge did not let anyone speak. Instead he sat and listened as the man spoke. He recognized the language the man was speaking. Other people in the court could also speak that language.

The judge didn't need to hear anything else. All charges against the man were dropped and the man was free to go.

A while later the same man was arrested again for holding a street meeting. In the court room he rebuked the lawyer in tongues!

For more than eight hours the jury tried to decide what to do. But they couldn't. In the end the man was released again without charge.

GOD IS MY LAWYER

Prentice was arrested for holding a street meeting. He was not well-educated, but he decided he did not need a lawyer. After all God was on his side.

As they chose the jury he read Matthew 10 several times. When he got to verses 14 and 15 he spoke them really clearly: *"If anyone will not welcome you or listen to your words, leave that home or town and shake the dust off your feet. Truly I tell you, it will be more bearable for Sodom and Gomorrah on the Day of Judgment than for that town"* (English Standard Version).

By the time they came to start the trial the judge did not want to try him and the prosecuting lawyer did not want to face him. "I am not going to stand against this man, even if you give me all the money in America. I am going to welcome him and listen to him." The case was dropped and Prentice was free to go.

Both the lawyer and the judge went to Azusa Street where they gave their lives to Jesus!

But not everybody got off so easily.

THE PRISON

Henry McClain had a wife and three young children. He was holding a prayer meeting in his home when the police came and knocked on his door. "You are disturbing the peace and making unusual noises." They said.

Henry was arrested and taken to court. The judge sentenced him to 30 days of hard labor in prison. But God hadn't left him. He had a bigger plan.

When Henry got to prison he met a lot of Mexicans there. He started to speak to them in tongues, not realizing that he was actually speaking their native language, Spanish. The Mexicans heard him speaking from Isaiah 55. Henry was not only speaking in a language he hadn't learned, he was speaking from a chapter in the Bible that he had never even read! (See Isaiah 55:1-13.)

By the time he finished speaking all the Mexicans were on the floor weeping and crying out to God.

THE PARHAM EFFECT

With so many people turning to Jesus you would have thought that the churches would be excited about what God was doing. But they weren't!

"These people are being tricked. This is not of God!" they cried out.

William Seymour was not bothered by what other church leaders were saying. He knew that he was doing what God wanted him to do.

But he was bothered by some of the things that were happening in Azusa Street. Some occultists kept trying to join the meetings and bring their evil practices in, and a few of the Christians were being pulled away from God by these occultists as they tried to introduce evil practices.

Some people were just showing off emotions, rather than allowing the Holy Spirit to choose when and how the gifts of the Spirit would be manifest among the people in the meetings. William kept on praying but he did not really know how to stop these things without stopping God from moving.

For a while now William had been writing to his Bible School teacher, Charles Parham to ask him to come and join them. Charles had promised to come, but he was busy elsewhere. Now William wrote to Charles again, begging him to come quickly to help sort out the mess.

When Charles finally came he spoke very strongly against the work, instead of helping William to sort out the problems. Charles spoke plainly to the gathering of people and William and the workers saying, "People are far too emotional here."

The emotionalism and the different races mixing together wasn't at all unusual for the little mission church on Azusa Street in Los Angeles, but it was unusual for people from Texas like Charles Parham.

In the end William locked the doors and stopped Charles from coming back in. William had always seen Charles as the father of the work in Azusa Street. Now the two of them were not even speaking to each other.

Charles tried to start up another revival work in the town, but it failed. He soon moved on to other things, leaving William to carry on.

William felt he needed to put more structure in place to keep the work together. But God's plan was to spread the work all over the world.

CHAPTER 14

SENT OUT

Street sign of Azusa Street where people came from all over the world.

SAVED TO SERVE

As people came through the Azusa Street mission, William Seymour encouraged them: "Don't just come to these meetings, live for God wherever you go."

People who were saved there brought others along, but this was just the first step.

William had been taught by Charles Parham that this move of the Holy Spirit was a missionary move. People who had been baptized should go out and share the Gospel with those who had never heard it.

And that's exactly what God wanted to happen.

Dianne was a young mom. She had two small children to look after and a huge lump on her head. The lump was half the size of a basketball. The doctors had told her that they could not operate on it because it was too big. They also told her that she was going to die soon.

She had heard how God was healing people in a mission house on Azusa Street, but she didn't really believe the stories. However she was now becoming desperate and said to herself, "I've got nothing to lose. I'm going to die anyway, so I may as well go along, in case the stories are true."

So one evening she slipped into the meeting with her two children by her side, and her hands surrounding and covering the huge lump on her head because she was so embarrassed. Before she could even get to her seat a crowd of people had surrounded her. They wanted to pray for her.

"God is going to heal you. You have come here for a miracle haven't you?"

Dianne didn't really believe God could heal her, but she had come for a miracle so she replied, "yes."

As they prayed the lump just disappeared. This was a start of a new life for Dianne. She gave her life to God and went on to start a soup kitchen and ministered to the poor and those who had no food.

Many other people continued to serve God for the rest of their lives. Some became pastors, others evangelists. Some simply lived for Jesus in their ordinary lives. The members of Azusa Street would carry a bottle of oil with them wherever they went so that they could anoint the sick with oil and pray for healing. Many went on to the streets to preach and worked hard to clothe the poor and feed the hungry. They wanted to show the Kingdom of God to people wherever they went.

And some of them went far, far away.

COMING FROM ALL OVER THE WORLD

As the work at Azusa Street grew, people started to hear about it all over the world. Charles Parham had called his church the Apostolic Faith Church so William labeled the work the Apostolic Faith Church too. People started to see this as one of Charles Parham's works.

Frank Bartleman wasn't very happy about this. He had been in the revival from the beginning. He had been in touch with Evan Roberts the Welsh revivalist who had helped pray this revival into place.

Now Frank thought people were trying to organize the revival instead of letting God be in charge. In August, 1906, he left and started up his own revival meetings at Eighth and Maple Streets in Los Angeles. And God moved there in power.

Meanwhile, back in Azusa Street the meetings were becoming more organized.

William started to produce a newsletter, called The Apostolic Faith, to let everyone know what God was doing. More and more people wanted to hear about this work. Before long 50,000 newsletters were being sent out each month.

Many people were healed when they touched the newsletters. Just like God's glory was carried through handkerchiefs that were brought to Paul in Acts, now His glory was being carried on these letters. (See Acts 19:12)

Some people didn't just want to read about what God was doing. They wanted to see it and be part of it for themselves.

People traveled from across America and from all over the world to see this move of God. Whatever they had heard about it before they came, they were even more amazed when they experienced it for themselves.

People came from Canada, Africa, Europe, China, Japan and India.

Many of them went home having received the Holy Spirit. They literally carried the revival back home.

GOING TO THE ENDS OF THE EARTH

Missionaries who came to Azusa Street helped to inspire others to go overseas. Some of the members of the Cambridge Seven, a well-known group of missionaries from England to China, spent a lot of time at Azusa Street.

The first missionary who went out traveled through Colorado, Illinois and New York before leaving for Spain, Jerusalem and Sweden.

In June, 1906, a pastor stood before the crowd. "I believe God is calling me to go to India." He had no money to go, but he did not tell people that. They did not even take up an offering. Instead God started to tell people to give.

One man stood up, "I will give you $500 to go."

Another stood to offer $100.

Fifteen minutes later enough money had been raised to send five people to India.

By October, 1906, the mission had officially sent out thirty missionaries to America and eight missionaries to the rest of the world. But this was just the beginning of a major missionary emphasis.

A few months later William told a friend, "We are sending somebody out as a missionary nearly every single day." Wherever the missionaries went they told people what had happened to them.

In Azusa Street many people went upstairs to the upper room to ask God to baptize them in the Holy Spirit. At any one time a hundred people would be there waiting on God. Throughout the revival time at Azusa Street, thousands came back down those stairs baptized in the Holy Spirit and speaking in tongues.

William had been taught that tongues would be used by God to spread the Gospel around the world. People would be given a language by God when they traveled overseas, so they wouldn't need to learn it.

Although there were a lot of times when people understood tongues, none of the missionaries ended up using tongues in this way.

But all of the missionaries went out wanting to see their converts baptized in the Holy Spirit in the same way as they had experienced. Having been in Azusa Street they did not just want to tell people about God, they wanted the people to encounter God for themselves.

Within two years, thousands of Pentecostal missionaries had been sent out. Many of them died on the mission field when they were young, but through them, the Pentecost experience with the Holy Spirit was established in over fifty different countries.

Some of the people who came to the Azusa Street Revival became well-known ministers and evangelists in the future.

John Lake spent time there before travelling out to South Africa to start a great work there. You can read his incredible story in God's Generals for Kid's: Volume 8 of this series.

Robert and Aimee Semple heard God call them to go to China as missionaries. Before they went Owen Adams came from Azusa Street. He told them all about what God was doing and they received the baptism of the Holy Spirit.

Unfortunately, Robert died soon after they arrived in China. Aimee came home and married Harold McPherson. Aimee Semple McPherson became one of the most famous Pentecostal preachers of her time and started the

International Church of the Foursquare Gospel. Her story is told in God's Generals for Kids: Volume 9 of this series.

Mr. Ward and Mr. Riggs were teenagers running around praying for the sick when the revival first began. They later helped to start the Assemblies of God churches, now the largest Pentecostal denomination in the world.

The Holy Spirit was being poured out in other places, but the work in Azusa Street seemed to spread around the world more than any other work that God had started.

As it continued to spread around, God had done what He wanted to do in that simple stable. Azusa Street had served its purpose.

CHAPTER 15

FALLING APART

William Seymour with his wife Jennie

JOIN ME

Elmer Fisher was a Baptist minister. When he came to Azusa Street he was baptized in the Holy Spirit.

For a few months he led the meetings at Azusa Street while William traveled around America to tell other people the message of Pentecost. When William came back Elmer wanted to carry on leading but William did not let him.

Frank Bartleman had already left Azusa Street and started his own meetings in August, 1906. Now Elmer left Azusa Street and started his own "Upper Room" meetings. Many of the white people left Azusa Street and joined him. George Studd, the brother of C.T. Studd a famous English missionary, also joined with Elmer.

Bit by bit the revival, where people had been so united, was now being split into pieces. It began only a few months after the revival had started. One person wrote: "Some say, 'We are with William Seymour', others say 'We are with Charles Parham,' and still others say 'We are with Frank Bartleman.'"

In the middle of all this mess, Elmer tried to keep people focusing on Jesus. Again and again he told his congregation: "Lift up Jesus Christ and honor the Holy Spirit."

IT'S OUR BUILDING

In 1907, the building at Azusa Street was still waiting to be sold. More and more people were buying land. People were worried that someone was going to buy their building so they decided to buy it first. But they did not have enough money.

William told the people what was needed and before long they had raised enough money to buy the whole building.

But some people weren't happy. William had broken an unspoken rule in Azusa Street—he had asked people for money.

Money had never even been mentioned in the mission before, everyone just trusted God. One of the elders said they needed to record every cent that was given and how it was spent. But William had never written anything down.

"I've just done what God told me to do with the money. Most of it was given to people who needed it, but I couldn't even tell you who I gave it to now. What I do know is that I have not wasted a single cent of God's money," he told the elder.

William lived on the edge of poverty, he owned no property and only just met his own needs. He was definitely not using the money for himself.

But the question had been asked because the people were trying to control God's work.

WEDDING BELLS

Jennie Moore had been the first lady to speak in tongues in Los Angeles. Jennie had played the piano beautifully having never learned to play it. Jennie had told other people about the move of God in Azusa Street. Jennie had been there from the very start.

It's no surprise that William and Jennie worked very closely together. What did surprise people was when William decided to marry her.

God was moving so powerfully that some people thought Jesus would be coming back within a year. They were so sure of it that they believed nobody should get married. After all there was too much work to do in the kingdom to be distracted by marriage.

William didn't agree. He taught about marriage. He showed the people that it was not a sin to get married. And then finally, on May 13, 1908, he married Jennie.

OPPOSITION WITHIN

One of William's friends had warned him that people may be upset. After all, although Jennie was black she was from Ethiopia.

"People from different races should not get married," he said.

Azusa Street had been famous for the way that the races mixed together, but this marriage was too much for some of the people to accept who lived at that time. It seemed like that acceptance was slipping away and as it did people left.

Claire Lunn ran away from the mission to Portland, Oregon. She had been one of William's faithful workers. When she left she took the address list for the newsletters with 50,000 names and addresses on. She carried on sending out the newsletter from Portland. Most people didn't realize that William now had nothing to do with it.

Suddenly William was left with no way of speaking to people who did not come to the meetings. Azusa Street would never be the same again.

Around this time William stopped putting his head in the top box of the pulpit. Whether God told him to stop, or whether he felt ashamed of it we will never know. But when he stopped putting his head inside the box, God's glory stopped coming as it had before.

Other people now set up meetings around Los Angeles and more of the people began to drift there. Before long no white people were coming to Azusa Street and the numbers of people attending were falling every week.

I DON'T AGREE WITH YOU

With less people coming, there was less money. With less money William decided it was time to go traveling. People all over the country had been asking him to come and speak to them. Now seemed like the right time to go.

In 1911, Pastor William H. Durham came and started to teach at Azusa Street. When Pastor Durham had been there in 1907, he had been baptized in the Holy Spirit and William had prophesied over him that God would use him to preach with the power of God. Now in 1911, Pastor Durham did just that.

People started to come back to the mission and it filled up again. People did not leave their seats between services in case someone else came and sat there. In one service over 500 people had to be turned away.

As Pastor Durham spoke he told people that the baptism of the Holy Spirit was the starting point for becoming holy. William believed that they were two separate works of God's grace. As soon as William heard what Pastor Durham was preaching he rushed back.

"Pastor Durham, please stop preaching in this way. This is not what we believe here."

But Pastor Durham didn't listen. He went out to the crowds and asked them: "Who wants me to be the leader here? And who wants me to let William Seymour be the leader?"

Today most people would agree with Pastor Durham's teaching. But very few people would agree that he should have tried to push William out of the church God had given him to lead. After all God tells us to honor our leaders. In the Bible, David honored King Saul even though Saul was trying to kill him.

When only ten people voted to keep William as the leader, he felt that he had no choice. He was the leader. God had given him the leadership. And he could not stop doing what God had called him to do.

That Sunday he padlocked the doors to the mission to stop Pastor Durham and his followers from coming in.

They continued to argue about different teachings. Can you lose you salvation? Or when you are saved do you stay saved forever? Is the teaching about trinity correct?

Instead of seeking God, William had somehow got distracted by these arguments.

In the past when people disagreed he would pray and let God sort it out. Even when people were against the work in Azusa he left it to God to sort out. Now he seemed to feel it was his job to make sure everything was right.

Pastor Durham did not try to preach in Azusa Street again. He found another building in Los Angeles and started holding meetings there. More people left Azusa Street and followed him to the new building.

By 1913, there were only twenty people left at Azusa Street and they only held one meeting a week on a Sunday. For two and a half years God had filled that building with His glory and thousands of people had come to meet God there. Now only twenty people were left.

The others hadn't stopped following God. They just didn't go to the meetings at Azusa Street. Instead they were spread across Los Angeles, America and the rest of the world. But none of them would ever forget their experiences in Azusa Street.

Charles Parham had been the first to teach so clearly on the baptism of the Spirit. When Charles had introduced this message God allowed him to fade into the background. William Seymour had learned from him and taught it to thousands of people. Now he had done this work God allowed him to fade into background. Thousands of people were given the task to spread this message further.

You see God's Kingdom does not depend on one person as the leader. God raises up people at different times to different jobs. That's why we have to be humble when God uses us. After all He can choose to use anyone whenever He wants to. If we realize that we don't know everything but God does, God will be able to use us more.

God loves to use people who are humble, but He stops using people who think they are the next big thing in His Kingdom. There is only one big thing in God's Kingdom and that is God himself.

In 1914, a group of ministers met together. Many of them had been part of the revival at Azusa Street but were no longer going there. They wanted to be united together and to support each other. They shared the same heart—heart they wanted to send out missionaries and see people filled with the Holy Spirit.

Lots of people were confused by different teachings that were going around. So these leaders also wanted to make sure that people got their teachings about God from the Bible. Together they started the Assemblies of God. Before long churches from all over America and around the world had joined them. Different nations started their own Assemblies of God groups and the churches grew.

CHAPTER 16

THE REST OF HIS LIFE

William Seymour as an old man

THE CLOSING YEARS

After all the divisions in the church, William was very sad. A lot of it had been because he was black. He could have chosen to hate the white people. After all, it looked like they had destroyed the unity in Azusa Street. The Holy Spirit was sad and moved on when the unity went.

But William knew that hating people doesn't help you or them. When you are full of hate only God can help you. After all, he would tell them, "There is no medicine for hate."

In 1918, William invited all of the Pentecostal leaders of Los Angeles to come to a meeting. He wanted everyone to talk about how they could join together in unity for God's Kingdom. Only two leaders came. William was very disappointed.

With only twenty people to look after at Azusa Street, William decided to travel across America again. But over time people were not that interested to hear from him. Some people came to see him and remembered the great move of God that had taken place at Azusa Street. Each time William was happy to meet with them again.

By now there were so few people at the mission that there was not enough money to pay the bills. Sometimes they had to take up two offerings. Jennie, Seymour's wife, got a job so that they could have enough money for food.

In 1921, William took one last ministry trip across America. When he came back home in 1922 people noticed that he looked very tired.

He went to many meetings and gatherings of leaders. But he was never mentioned from the platform. It seemed like this great man of God had been forgotten already by the thousands he had helped.

On September 28, 1922, William felt a sharp pain in his chest. One of the workers ran to get the doctor. The doctor came to examine him and told him to rest.

At 5 p.m. that afternoon, while he was sitting dictating a letter he felt another strong pain. He struggled to breathe and then went to be with Jesus. He was only fifty-two years old.

On his gravestone they simply wrote "Our Pastor." Only two hundred people came to his funeral even though thousands had been touched by his life. But in Heaven God saw all of his work and he is now getting his reward for it.

LIFE AT AZUSA STREET

After William died, Jennie Seymour became the leader of the small group. In 1931, the council said that the building was a fire hazard and no more meetings could be held there. Azusa Street Mission had officially closed, but the effects of that mission still continue.

Five years later Mrs. Jennie Seymour suffered from heart failure just like William had. On July 2, 1936, she went to Heaven.

A MOVE OF GOD

God moved through William Seymour and the other believers in Azusa Street in a very special way. They saw amazing miracles. You could literally touch God's presence in that little church on Azusa Street. Thousands of people were being saved. And people were going out around the whole world to preach the Gospel.

The Pentecostal group of churches is still the fastest growing part of the Christian church in the world and most of the Pentecostal Churches and the Charismatic Churches today can trace their roots back to Azusa Street. The Assemblies of God and Full Gospel Businessmen's fellowship are just two of the large organizations that came out of the revival in Azusa Street.

But God was the one who was over the work at Azusa Street. William Seymour was used by God as he spent hours in prayer and knew that he needed God. William did not want people to look to him, instead he wanted them to seek God. When people look for God, God moves.

Many of the leaders at the time prophesied that there would be another great move of God in around one hundred years' time.

That's now.

Would you like to be a part of a move of God like Azusa Street? Would you like to see God work through you like He did through the people in Azusa Street?

God is looking for people who are willing to follow Him no matter what other people say, even if it means putting your head in a box! William Seymour decided to obey God, whatever God told him to do. Will you do the same?

Pray and ask God to move. Meet with other people and pray with them. And keep on praying. William prayed for many hours a day for several years before God used him at Azusa Street. Many others spent hours in prayer to get ready.

They did not regret it and you won't regret it either!

BIBLE STUDY FOR YOUNG GENERALS

Read Galatians 3:26-29

1. What do you think it means to put on (or be clothed with) Christ?

2. How does being baptized in the Holy Spirit help you to put on Christ?

3. The Apostle Paul, who wrote the book of Galatians, said that there were no slaves or free, Jew or Gentile. In William Seymour's time Azusa Street got rid of the barriers between races, classes and ages. What barriers do you think we need to get rid of between people today so that we remember that we are all equal before God?

4. What does it mean to be an heir to God (or to inherit from God)?

WILLIAM SEYMOUR —ACTIVITY SECTION

REMEMBER THE BOOK

How much of the story can you remember? Test your memory by answering these questions.

Answers are given on page 124.

1. What did William's parents do for a living?
2. How old was William when he left home to work?
3. Where did William have to sit when he went to Charles Parham's Bible school?
4. What street became the main meeting place for the revival?
5. How could God's glory be seen in the revival?
6. What was the Carney rule?

CHOOSE THE RIGHT ANSWER

Answers are given on page 124.

1. How did William lose his sight in one eye?

   A. Measles

   B. A mining accident

   C. Small pox

2. Which city did William travel to expecting revival to start?

   A. Texas

   B. Los Angeles

   C. New York

3. How did the revival start?

   A. Church meetings

   B. Street preaching

   C. Prayer meetings

4. Which miracles took place in the revival?

   A. Blind eyes see

   B. An ear grows back

   C. Lame people walk

5. In the height of the revival how often were new missionaries sent out?

A. Daily

B. Weekly

C. Monthly

6. After the revival how many people came to Azusa Street each week?

A. 20

B. 200

C. 2000

ANSWERS

1. They were slaves, 2. 13, 3. Outside the door of the classroom, 4. Azusa Street, 5. People did not want to leave, cloud filling the building, salvation, miracles, fire on the roof, all races mixing together., 6. "If you expect God to heal the person then you better get them ready for the healing: take off the braces, remove the footrests from the wheelchair."

1. C, 2. B, 3. C, 4. A, B & C, 5. A, 6. A.

AROUND THE WORLD

The people from Azusa Street travelled all over the word to share the Gospel. Time yourself to find out how quickly can you find some of the places they went to on a map or globe, *in the order they are written*:

1.	Canada	5.	Japan
2.	South Africa	6.	India
3.	China	7.	Sweden
4.	Spain	8.	Israel

Write down your times here.

Date	Time Taken

PUZZLE IT

Cross out all of the letters B, C, F, O and S in the grid below. Then write the remaining letters on the lines below in the order they appear to find three key parts of the revival in Azusa Street.

B	U	B	N	F	B	I	T
F	O	Y	P	S	R	C	O
A	C	S	C	Y	S	F	S
S	C	E	O	S	B	R	C
F	A	B	O	N	F	S	B
O	O	D	S	B	B	H	S
U	C	S	M	I	C	O	L
O	I	B	T	B	Y	C	F

_ _ _ _ _   _ _ _ _ _ _

_ _ _   _ _ _ _ _ _ _ _

FIND IT OUT

Plants need the right environment to grow in. Healthy plants then produce seeds to spread more flowers around. In the same way Azusa Street became a place of faith were lots of people travelled all over the world carrying the seed of all they had seen in Azusa Street.

Growing plants needs the right environment.

YOU WILL NEED

- 3 pots
- Cotton wool
- Cress seeds
- Water
- Ruler

WHAT TO DO

1. Put cotton wool into each of the three pots and add water.
2. Place 10 water cress seeds in each pot on the cotton wool evenly spread out.
3. Place all 3 pots on a window ledge until the seeds begin to sprout (germinate).
4. Then place one pot in a dark cupboard, one in a shaded part of the house, and leave one on the window ledge.
5. Keep the cotton wool damp with water.
6. Each day for one week measure the height of each seedling and work out the average (mean) height for each pot.

QUESTIONS TO THINK ABOUT

1. Why was it important to keep one of the plants in the light for this experiment?
2. What does faith need to grow?
3. What do the seeds of faith produce?

FOR FURTHER RESEARCH

1. What do plants need to grow? Create experiments like the one above to test how water and fresh air are needed to help plants grow. Does it matter if the seeds are close together or spread out? You will need to keep one pot in the best conditions this is called a control. Read up about controls in experiments to find out more.
2. How do plants spread their seeds?
3. Find out how some plants have been created to survive in hard conditions—for example in the desert or the arctic.
4. Read Jesus' stories about seeds and think about what they mean.

YOUR TURN

William Seymour spent hours in prayer before and during the revival. Having read how God can use someone who is fully devoted to Him, would you like to devote yourself to God in the same way? Start to grow your prayer life today. Set a time for 30 minutes or an hour and spend that time in prayer.

GET CREATIVE

William Seymour was in contact with Charles Parham (see page 139), his Bible teacher. Evan Roberts the Welsh Revivalist also wrote to the people in Azusa Street (see page 29). Recreate a letter that he might have written.

YOU WILL NEED

• Cup of hot coffee or hot tea

• A sheet of paper

• A pen

• A tray

• A hair dryer

WHAT TO DO

1. Make a cup of coffee or tea (with your parents' permission) and leave it to cool a bit.
2. Tear off the edges of the paper to create a rough edge to the letter.
3. Screw the paper up into a tight ball and then flatten it out again.
4. Place the paper on a tray and cover it in the coffee or tea.
5. Leave it to soak for 5 minutes.
6. Dry with a hair dryer.
7. Write the letter using the pencil (don't forget to put a date on the letter).
8. Admire your work.

EXTRA IDEA

Why not make an envelope for your letter and research how you can create a wax seal for your envelope (make sure your parents are with you when you do this).

AUTHORS' NOTE TO READERS AND PARENTS

Like William Seymour, I believe that God can cure people miraculously today. However, I do not believe that this is the only way that God will work. God gives wisdom and knowledge to us to help us fight disease. Medicine has advanced much since the time of William Seymour. Medical care can actually be part of God's plan for bringing relief and healing to His people. However, medicine still does not hold all the answers. I am in favor of both competent medical treatment and the power of prayer. I would not encourage anyone to neglect either of these at their time of need.

BIBLIOGRAPHY

Frank Bartleman, *The Azusa Street Revival Eyewitness Account* (Los Angeles, CA: 1925)

Roberts Liardon, *God's Generals: Why They Succeeded and Why Some Failed* (Tulsa, OK: Whitaker House 1996)

Larry E. Martin, *The Life and Ministry of William Seymour* (Pensacola, FL: Christian Life Books 1999)

Rufus Sanders, *William Joseph Seymour: Black Father of the 20th Century Pentecostal/Charismatic Movement* (Sandusky, OH: Xulon Press 2003)

Tommy Welchel, *They Told Me Their Stories* (USA, Dare2Dream Books 2008)

AUTHORS' CONTACT INFORMATION

ROBERTS LIARDON

Roberts Liardon Ministries, United States office:

P.O. Box 781888, Orlando, FL 32878

E-mail: Info1@robertsliardon.org

www.robertsliardon.org

United Kingdom/European office:

Roberts Liardon Ministries

22 Notting Hill Gate, Suite 125

London W11 3JE, UK

OLLY GOLDENBERG

BM Children Can, London WC1N 3XX, UK

info@childrencan.co.uk

www.childrencan.co.uk

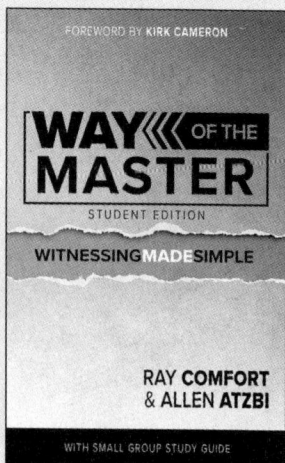